Old Kingussie and Bader
with Newtonmore and Dalwhinr
by Ann Glen

In 1908 Baden-Powell's book *Scouting for Boys* launched the Boy Scout movement and troops were formed throughout the country. The Kingussie Troop was founded in 1909 by A.M. Macintyre, the janitor and drill teacher in the local school who became Scoutmaster. Support from King Edward VII and the nobility soon gave Scouting status and the Clan Chief Cluny Macpherson became County Commissioner for Inverness-shire. Pictured here in 1912, the boys of the Kingussie Troop are out on patrol with their pet goat. The Kingussie and Newtonmore Troops have since combined to form the Badenoch Troop.

© Ann Glen, 2008

First published in the United Kingdom, 2008,
reprinted 2014,
by Stenlake Publishing Ltd.
www.stenlake.co.uk
ISBN 9781840334388

The publishers regret that they cannot supply
copies of any pictures featured in this book.

Acknowledgements

The following are thanked for providing information which has been helpful in researching material for this book: George A. Dixon; Walter Dempster; Cameron Ormiston; Hamish Johnstone; Lesley Kettle; Patrick Thompson; and Ian Chadbury, secretary of Kingussie Golf Club. The staff at Highland Council Archives and the National Archives of Scotland are also thanked for their assistance. Additional images have kindly been made available by John Robertson (page 39) and by Newtonmore Golf Club (page 19). John Peter has prepared all the photographs for publication. The publishers wish to thank the author for contributing the photographs on pages 2, 5, 10, 12, 13, 16, 20, 21, 23, 28, 29, 44, 45 and 47

At 1,160 feet above sea level, Dalwhinnie claims to be the highest village in the Highlands. Lying in the open valley of Glen Truim, it is exposed to winter's blizzards. This photograph shows the village's Loch Ericht Hotel after such an event in February 1940 when trains were snowed in on Druimuachdar Pass. A notorious area on the line was 'The Bachan', a cutting south of the village. Local people have been known to leave their houses through snow tunnels at front doors or climb from first floor windows. There is a Meteorological Station at Dalwhinnie Distillery.

INTRODUCTION

Badenoch is an ancient name for the district drained by the upper waters of the River Spey and its tributaries such as the Truim, the Tromie, the Gynack and the Feshie. The name itself means 'the drowned land' and any view from high ground makes sense of that choice. There is a marked contrast between the flat valley floors and the mountains; between these lie undulating terraces, safe above the flood plains. Rising beyond are steep slopes merging into plateau summits with the high Cairngorms on the east flank and the Monadhliath Mountains on the west. Badenoch can boast mighty lochs in Loch Ericht and Loch Laggan, but it also has Loch Insh through which the Spey flows, sheltered Loch Alvie and several others.

At the Pass of Druimuachdar, Badenoch marches with Atholl – the smooth-backed hills bordering the pass being known as the Sow of Atholl and the Boar of Badenoch. On the west lies Lochaber and on the east the Forest of Mar. To the north Strathspey begins where the rocky bluff of Craigellachie rises at Aviemore. So, Badenoch is physically well defined and its special identity can be sensed.

From early times tribal groups or clans claimed Badenoch, believing that their ancestors were first to occupy it. By the Middle Ages the Comyn family of Norman descent held it in feudal control, but in the thirteenth century they were overthrown. Eventually Robert II chose to hand the territory over to his illegitimate son, Alexander, Earl of Buchan. Known as the 'Wolf of Badenoch', he had a fearsome reputation and his stronghold was on a mound above the marshes at Ruthven. In the mid-fifteenth century the Earls of Huntly, later Dukes of Gordon, were the largest and most powerful landowners in the district. Even so, the Clan Macpherson was a major force in Badenoch.

Below the chief were tacksmen who were often relations. Then came clansmen working plots of land in townships, or 'baile', for which they paid rent in kind. They grazed livestock on the hill pastures in summer and cut peat on the mosses for fuel. Harvests were meagre due to continuous cropping and adverse weather. For clan folk this meant survival at

subsistence level and starvation was not unknown. The chief had authority to administer laws and to call out men to protect clan interests – in fact, his power centred on their number and his wealth was dependent on the cattle in the herds. Hides, horn and wool were items in a limited trade.

By the seventeenth century the Civil War brought conflict between Royalists and Covenanters. In the 1680s Ruthven Castle was burned down and the armies of both factions crossed Badenoch. By 1715 the first Jacobite rising put the Highlands in turmoil and in its aftermath Ruthven was repaired and Independent Highland Companies were recruited ostensibly to check cattle thieving. Highland security was a concern and Major-General George Wade's investigations pointed to 'the want of roads and bridges'. Though the purpose of the military roads was strategic, namely to join up fortresses, they also changed the locational value of Badenoch. Rough tracks were replaced by surfaces capable of taking wheeled vehicles and Ruthven became a government barracks.

The 1745 Jacobite rising under Prince Charles Edward Stuart was a turning point in the Highlands. In February 1746 his army crossed Badenoch *en route* to Culloden; after defeat, survivors retreated to Ruthven and left the barracks a blazing ruin. The government then suppressed opposition ruthlessly; tartan and bagpipes were proscribed and the power of the chiefs was curtailed. For many landowners and their families, wealth in money and honours gained in the south or the expanding empire came to mean more than their hereditary rights and responsibilities.

By the 1760s, the age of improvement had begun. Lairds, eager for income, promoted land reclamation and the use of lime to counteract acid soils. The new settlement of Kingussie ('Ceann a' Ghuibhsaich', pronounced 'king-you-sie' and meaning 'the head of the pine woods') was planned and in the 1800s tradesmen, manufacturers and shopkeepers were encouraged to take up plots there. However, when sheep farming was widely introduced, reorganisation of the land – replacing townships with individual farms – resulted in people being cleared from the clachans. It was in these circumstances that Newtonmore began to grow. There were waves of emigration too; in 1833 eighty people were proposing to leave for America.

Kingussie emerged as the capital of Badenoch; it had a parish church and soon there were schools and a library, while several markets were held each year. By the 1840s lairds were finding that land for shooting game was a marketable commodity and grouse moors were supplemented with vast deer forests. The business was 'splendidly profitable'. Some estates were split into 'ranges' for leasing to the wealthy and many shooting lodges were constructed up to 1914.

In 1863 the railway came to Badenoch, bringing middle class families attracted to the fresh mountain environment and healthful pine-scented air. Villas were built for rental by the month and many hotels were opened. There was an expansion of services – more shops, churches and halls appeared and golf courses were set out. It was a prosperous phase cut short by the disaster of the First World War. The memorials erected after 1918 are witness to the scale of the tragedy.

The interwar years brought uncertainty and economic depression. Even so, with popular tourism based on cars, motor traffic soared; holidaymakers were more mobile than ever before and caravans appeared on the new Great North Road. During the Second World War Badenoch became part of a training ground for combat and the lodges were commandeered by the military. Farming to feed the nation was on a high but visitor numbers shrank.

From the 1950s, sports holidays and skiing made some impact in encouraging tourism in Badenoch. Then in the early 1980s, the route of the new A9 trunk road left the key town of Kingussie and villages from Dalwhinnie to Kincraig bypassed. There were mixed opinions about this outcome – on the one hand a notable easing of traffic congestion, noise and pollution, especially when traffic was heavy in summer, was welcomed, but on the other there were concerns about the inevitable loss of trade to local businesses. Badenoch's communities have also felt shortchanged when seeing the scale of investment in private housing, resort development and other facilities – notably the Cairngorm Mountain Railway – focused on the Aviemore area.

However, there have also been developments in the Badenoch villages and two major projects, the Highland Folk Museum at Newtonmore and the Highland Wildlife Park near Kincraig, come to mind. In addition, the TV series *Monarch of the Glen*, by highlighting Badenoch's many qualities, is credited with helping to redress the balance and draw visitors to explore the district for themselves. Although extensive sporting estates continue, the economic and social contribution of outdoor activities such as hill walking, mountaineering, mountain biking, kayaking, sailing and pony trekking is estimated to far outweigh these in terms of local benefits. Increasingly too, tourists escaping the heat of continental summers and aware of climate change speak of finding respite in quiet, green, refreshing Badenoch and its friendly villages.

Further Reading

The books listed below were used by the author during her research. None are available from Stenlake Publishing; please contact your local bookshop or reference library.

Ann Glen, *The Cairngorm Gateway*, Scottish Cultural Press, 2002.
I.F. Grant, *Highland Folkways, Routledge & Kegan Paul*, 1961.
M. Marshall, *Glen Feshie, The History and Archeology of a Highland Glen*, NOSAS Publication, 2006.
O.S. Nock, *The Highland Railway*, Ian Allan, 1965.
J. & U. Robertson, *Kingussie, Caught in the Light*, Kingussie Millennium Committee, 1999.
J. & U. Robertson, *Kingussie, Lasting Impressions*, Kingussie Arts Network, 2006.

W. Taylor, *The Military Roads of Scotland*, House of Lochar, 1996.
A. Wightman, *Who Owns Scotland*, Canongate, 1996.
The *Statistical Account of Scotland* (1791–99) and the *New Statistical Account of Scotland* (1834–45), the *Ordnance Gazetteer of Scotland* (1892), the valuation rolls for Inverness-shire, and back issues of the *Kingussie Advertiser*, the *Badenoch Record*, and the *Strathspey Herald* were also consulted.

Loch Ericht is 15 miles long and is thus one of the largest freshwater surfaces in the Highlands. It is dammed at its southern end for hydro-electricity where a tunnel aqueduct conveys water to a power station on Loch Rannoch. There is also a dam on the north end from which the Cuaich Power Station is supplied. These installations were originally planned as part of the Grampian Electricity Supply Company's scheme of 1930 and completed in 1961. The result has been the raising of the level of the loch and the submergence of the area seen here, once a 'stance' where livestock could be watered, grazed or be fed overnight during cattle-droving days.

In 1863 the Inverness & Perth Junction Railway was completed through the Grampian Mountains. Within two years, the Highland Railway was in charge and continued so for sixty years. It was a major employer; here the stationmaster, signalman, porters, lamp boy and clerks pose on the 'up' platform at Dalwhinnie. As this village stands high, winter conditions could be severe and the signal wires were on posts above ground level to prevent damage. During the Second World War, General Montgomery's 'Rapier' train stood in a siding here in May 1944 while he relaxed among the hills prior to D-Day.

Dalwhinnie

On an Ordnance Survey map of 1872, 'Loch Ericht Lodge' is shown at this site five miles south-west of Dalwhinnie. However, twenty years later the name 'Ben Alder Lodge' was also being used. Once Macpherson territory and reckoned to have the best natural meadow in Badenoch, the land became a sheep run in the early 1800s. This proved unprofitable and by 1838 Ben Alder deer forest had been created; fifty years later this was being rented out at £2,650 a year, a phenomenal amount at that time. The old Ben Alder Lodge was demolished in 1993 and an elaborate replacement in Portuguese granite and other matching buildings have arisen by the lochside. The estate, extending to over 27,000 acres, is owned by Swiss interests and the Hanbury family.

In 1897 when the Scotch whisky business was booming and distilling seemed a good investment, this establishment was erected in Dalwhinnie for three local men including Alexander Mackenzie, the Kingussie architect who designed it. Known as the Strathspey Distillery, there was good water, plenty of peat and the railway conveyed barley, casks and coal to a siding. Every process from malting (note the pagoda-like kiln) to warehousing was done on the site. In 1899 the boom collapsed and the company stopped trading. In 1905 the name was changed to 'Dalwhinnie'. Trading difficulties brought several changes of ownership until the Distillers Company Ltd took over in 1926. Dalwhinnie was assigned to James Buchanan & Company, blenders of 'Black & White' whisky, but run by Scottish Malt Distillers Ltd, the pot still arm of DCL. Scarcities of grain in the Second World War caused closure. However, in 1943 Dalwhinnie was the first malt whisky distillery in Scotland to resume production, Prime Minister Winston Churchill – who liked a dram – realising that Scotch whisky takes years to mature. Between 1992 and 1995, £3.2 million was spent on total refurbishment by current owners United Distillers & Vintners, part of Diageo. The whisky is now marketed as a 'classic malt'.

LOCH ERICHT HOTEL, DALWHINNIE   A 2072

Beginning in the 1700s, possibly as a whisky howff serving cattle drovers bound for trysts at Crieff and Falkirk, Dalwhinnie soon lay on General Wade's military roads which first met here in 1729. By 1818 after Telford's road improvements, there was an inn which grouse-shooting toffs had to share with drovers. Queen Victoria and Prince Albert lodged here 'incognito' in 1847. The railway came in 1863, bringing many more visitors, and the inn was enlarged to become the Loch Ericht Hotel. By 1928 it stood beside the Great North Road, having an Automobile Association endorsement and petrol pumps.

GRAMPIAN HOTEL, DALWHINNIE.

The Grampian Hotel was a roadhouse at Dalwhinnie, replacing the Truim Bank Hotel which had been destroyed by fire in 1929. Built in 1941 to serve motorists on the A9 Great North Road, the hotel's modernist architecture 'stuck out like a sore thumb' amid the moors and mountains, and its opening in wartime was badly timed. Innovations such as the large windows, lounge and cocktail bar, sunroom and rooftop terrace were a break with the past. In the 1960s an extra storey was added in the hope that ski tourism would develop in the area. Sold on in 1985, by the latter 1990s only the bar remained in use. The structure was demolished in 2005.

Dalwhinnie

As motoring grew in popularity in the 1920s, the needs of motorists for petrol, oils and servicing had to be met. Garages or 'motor car sheds' were put up at hotels and 'motor mechanics' advertised their skills. The motoring boom also saw many roadside tearooms established to refresh travellers. The Grampian Tea Rooms at Dalwhinnie were housed in a recent addition to a small villa and provided a welcome stop for motorists before or after tackling the perils of the Pass of Druimuachdar in the days when cars had no heating. The adjacent garage offered repair facilities and a field was available for caravans, a new development in the interwar years. Now there are few Highland petrol outlets, yet vehicle ownership has never been greater.

The name 'Dail Chuinnidh' is Gaelic for the meeting place, in this case an ancient focus of routes north into Strathspey, south over Druimuachdar Pass and west to Lochaber. From 1725 General Wade's military roads brought further activity to Dalwhinnie and an inn was established where cattle drovers gathered. In 1863 the railway came along but at 1,160 feet winters were often severe. In this photograph, lengths of snow fencing are protecting the railway line alongside council housing, newly built by 1950. Overlooked by grouse moors and deer forests, the village's pot still distillery can be seen on the far left, and the Grampian Hotel is in the middle distance.

12   **Dalwhinnie**

The Spey Bridge at Ralia was an impressive structure built to the orders of the Duke of Gordon; the contract dates from 1763 and local people were obliged 'to hew & bring the Stones & Lime' for its construction. It cost £1,500 and was part of the military's Etteridge–Kerrowmeanach bypass of Ruthven, the barracks there having been destroyed by the Jacobites in 1746. When the Great North Road of 1925–28 was constructed, this old bridge (photographed here in 1892) was dismantled and a modern concrete one erected in its place.

The Inverness & Perth Junction Railway completed its line through the Grampians in 1863. The portion from Aviemore to Pitlochry saw its first trains for the public on 9 September of that year. From the outset, there was a timber station at Newtonmore but it subsequently burned down. This stone building with a veranda, in the typical Highland Railway style, was constructed in 1892 and is seen in its post-Second World War British Railways days. After 1965 the signal box and goods shed were demolished and the station is now a private house. However, eight trains a day continue to call at Newtonmore; using the same platform, there is now merely a simple shelter for passengers.

With the bridging of the Spey in 1765, a hamlet began along the road north. The *Statistical Account of Scotland* of 1791–99 describes how proper villages were lacking in Badenoch and how dwellings were 'mean, ill-constructed huts'. By the 1820s 'Newtown of the Moor' was accommodating folk cleared from townships on account of sheep farming at Phones, Etteridge, Ruthven and Glen Banchor. In the 1850s, emigration saw more people leave. However, the railway of 1863 brought summer visitors whose wealth and spending power transformed Newtonmore. Along Main Street, new buildings were erected, trades established and shops opened; by the 1890s, the fruiterer, grocer and provision merchant (left) also combined a house-letting agency.

Looking north-west across Newtonmore's Main Street, the Temperance Hotel is prominent in the foreground. The Temperance Movement was a major social force in the nineteenth century, when problems of drunkenness were widespread with consequent degradation and violence blighting communities. Families or women on holiday, and many people travelling on business, wished to have accommodation away from 'the demon drink' and temperance establishments were opened throughout Scotland. By the early 1900s most cottages along Main Street had been reconstructed from the 1800s originals, several villas had been built, and a parish church erected (far right). Local authority housing has since been sited in the fields to the rear of the

In this view the rocky slopes of Creag Dubh rise beyond the valley of the temperamental River Calder. It was in a cave on these slopes that the Clan Chief Cluny Macpherson hid after the defeat of the Jacobite army at Culloden in 1746. Banchor Mains Farm, with its large steading and offices, is in the centre of the photograph; it was harvest time when it was taken and the oats sheaves, set in stooks in line with the prevailing wind to dry the grain, seem to have suffered from the weather. By the early 1900s there was a contrast in styles between the modest cottage by the side of the A86 Laggan Road and the then-recently built, and rather grand, Glen Banchor Lodge on the right. Note the old speed limit sign in the foreground and the telegraph poles along the road.

The Balavil Arms Hotel, seen here in the distance, was built opposite a market stance at Newtonmore's north-east end in 1900. Several buildings on the approaching roadside have since been demolished and the sites redeveloped. The hotel was for long owned by the Ormiston family and it was here that Ewan and Cameron Ormiston pioneered sports holidays, beginning with pony trekking in 1952. The hotel also became popular with skiers during the Cairngorm winter sports boom of the 1960s. The family sold it between 1977 and 1980, although it is still in business as part of the McKever group. The Ormistons also had, and continue to have, farming interests in Badenoch, including the breeding of Highland cattle. Through six generations, since the 1850s when they came from East Lothian to work on the estate in Glen Feshie, their name has become synonymous with champion Highland ponies.

Newtonmore Golf Course was established in 1893 on rough grazing east of the village. Beginning with a few holes, by 1904 a clubhouse had been built. In 1909 a crowd gathered to see Arnaud Mass (centre, in light jacket), the first overseas player to win the Open Championship (1907), play a foursome. Described as 'the Frenchman with the soul of a Scot', he had outstanding records in the Open for two decades. After the First World War, James Braid, another Open champion, introduced course improvements, especially altering bunkers. Now 6,041 yards long, Newtonmore's varied holes test players including 'left handers', often with a shinty background, who have their own tournament.

Newtonmore from Spey Bridge

By the 1920s, with motoring increasing, there were frequent complaints about the condition of the Great North Road, little altered from Telford's time – just a strip of grit, stones and deep ruts, tarred only in places. Repairs meant filling potholes with crushed rock. Goods traffic was rising as cartage by horses over any distance declined. Then, in 1925, a new 20-feet-wide highway at £1,000 per mile with proper surfacing ('macadamisation') was proposed, allowing speeds of 25 mph in comfort. This ultramodern concrete bridge superseded the eighteenth-century structure at Ralia south of Newtonmore, but it only serves local access now. The Eilan, Newtonmore's shinty ground, is seen in the middle distance.

By the 1920s visitors increasingly looked for sports facilities when choosing places for family holidays – fresh air and exercise were appreciated as healthful. Besides, such pursuits were 'something to do', especially for youngsters, and tournaments brought visitors and local people together. If highland resorts such as Newtonmore were to retain their attractiveness they had to have these facilities. Tennis became popular through newspaper publicity about the 'star players' at Wimbledon. After strenuous fund raising by communities, many tennis courts and bowling greens were made in the interwar years. There was a blaes court on this site in Newtonmore in the early 1930s, replaced by an all-weather version in 1948. The bowling club was established in 1947. After a lean phase in the 1960s when the tennis courts were used for curling, fresh interest and investment revived them and both facilities remain in use.

Gaick lodge lies in the Gaick Pass which links Dalnacardoch with the Minigaig route to Glen Tromie. Gaick has a dark past. In January 1800 Captain John Macpherson of Ballachroan, known as the 'Black Officer', ventured with four companions to hunt in Gaick, spending the night in a hut there. It was overwhelmed by an avalanche from the steep hillsides and all of them perished. Macpherson was notorious as a recruiting officer inveigling youths into the Highland regiments and the episode was interpreted as a judgement. A replacement lodge was soon built near the head of Loch an t-Seilich. This has been modernised for letting and is 12 miles from Kingussie.

Cluny Castle, a classical villa with castellated trimmings, was built in 1805. Seat of the Chief of Clan Macpherson, the estate had been forfeited and the old house burned in 1746 on account of the chief's loyalty to the Jacobite cause. Cluny Macpherson spent nine years in hiding as a fugitive, then escaped to France in 1765 and never returned to Scotland. In 1784 the lands were given back to his descendants. The porch was added in 1891 and a wing in 1908. The estate has been sold off but a clan rallying ground has been retained and a Macpherson gathering is held annually. The castle is now in Norwegian ownership.

ARDVERIKIE LODGE FROM LOCH LAGGAN

Ardverikie is an imposing hunting lodge on the south shore of Loch Laggan. In 1844 the Duke of Abercorn leased the estate for hunting from the Clan Chief Cluny Macpherson; a new wing was built for a visit of Queen Victoria in 1847. The lease later passed to Sir John William Ramsden, a wealthy industrialist from West Yorkshire. As owner, he spent lavishly on improving the estate but regrettably the original house burned down in 1871, as did its replacement. However, Ramsden then built another grand house, the present mansion, first occupying it in 1877. This sporting estate and lodge later became well known through the TV drama *Monarch of the Glen*.

In 1804 the Duke of Gordon, the Macintosh of Macintosh and Cluny Macpherson urged the Commissioners for Highland Roads and Bridges to construct a road from the Inn at Pitmain in Badenoch via the north side of Loch Laggan to Fort William. Forty-two miles long, this difficult route was engineered by Thomas Telford and eventually completed in 1818. It cost five times more than estimated. Cameron's Inn at Kinloch Laggan, 15 miles from Pitmain, was a welcoming hostelry on the road and in 1902 it was enlarged to form the Loch Laggan Hotel, seen here.

Loch Laggan

FEEDING DEER, FOOT OF CORRIEARRICK

By 1731 the pass now known as Corrieyairack – a popular trek for long-distance walkers – was the route for General Wade's military road from Fort Augustus to Ruthven Barracks. In the 1860s, with the building of Sherramore Lodge, it belonged to the area taken up by the Sherramore deer forest. Here, one of the forest keepers is feeding hinds; this practice, which continues in winter on some estates, is meant to keep animals in good condition and ensure high densities for hunting. Without natural predators, there are estimated to be over 500,000 red deer in Scotland, double the number forty years ago. The estate, which is owned by Rio Tinto's Alcan Aluminium PLC, is now named Glenshero.

By the early 1890s, when this photograph was taken from Creag Bheag, Kingussie was growing fast with many new buildings in evidence. Lower left, in the Gynack valley, is an old wauk mill, while upper left is the parish church of 1792. In the centre is the High Street from which Ruthven Road, King Street and Duke Street branch off east in a grid pattern. On the right, the tallest building is the free church of 1877–79 while the school of 1874/75 is just below it on the same side of the street. The railway station is at the right edge of the photograph. The initial Duke of Gordon Hotel and villas in large gardens occupy the lower right, while the foreground would soon be taken up by the Speyside distillery of 1895. Meadowlands towards the Spey have been embanked, drained and are under cultivation.

In 1893 the Highland Railway replaced its timber-built station at Kingussie, dating from 1863, with a more commodious and elaborate stone building. Before trains had toilets or dining facilities, comfort calls were made at Kingussie, and so from an early date 'refreshment rooms' were opened in the timber building on the southbound platform (background left). The new premises, with the booking office and waiting rooms, are seen on the northbound platform (right). The footbridge was made to a standard HR pattern in the Rose Street Foundry at Inverness. The signal box (left) controlled the signals and level crossing on Ruthven Road.

Kingussie arose as a planned settlement on land owned by the Duke of Gordon with feus or plots going up for sale in 1799 on a grid plan. 'Tradesmen, Manufacturers and Shop-keepers' were encouraged to settle. Woollen manufacturing, using waterpower from the fast flowing River Gynack, a tributary of the Spey, was a prospect. The Gynack valley is on the right of the photograph. A tweed mill had some success upstream but this wauk mill for shrinking cloth became disused in 1899 and was converted to grind grain. The tweed mill is now named The Cross, an award-winning restaurant with some accommodation for visitors, while the grain mill has become a dwelling house.

In 1895 the Speyside Distillery – the premises in the foreground of this photograph of Kingussie – were constructed during a Scotch whisky boom. In 1899 the speculation stopped, the whisky 'bubble' burst, and the industry went into decline. Many distilleries closed at that time and a second blow came with the Lloyd George budget of 1909, which put a heavy duty on spirits. This distillery, with its fine buildings and rail connection, was soon abandoned. It was demolished and the rubble used as road bottoming for the new 'Great North Road' of the 1920s. Only former office accommodation and some housing stands today, but a small distillery, opened at Drumguish in 1991, uses the name 'Speyside' for its malt whisky.

The Duke of Gordon Hotel at the south end of Kingussie began as a new inn, dating from 1838. In 1906 rebuilding involved a design by Alexander Cattanach, a local architect. This was an initiative by the local landowner and director of the Highland Railway, James Baillie of Dochfour. (He was married to the heiress to the Bass brewery fortune, who became Baroness Burton of Burton-on-Trent.) From 'The Duke', as the hotel was known, the horse-drawn mail coach 'Duchess of Gordon' set out for Tulloch until the service was withdrawn in 1908 (that year it had become the last horse-drawn mail service in Britain). The hotel was damaged by fire in 1999 but has since been reconstructed.

As the Duke of Gordon was the premier hotel in Badenoch in the Edwardian years, this drawing room reflected the 'haute bourgeois' taste which was popular at that time. The lavish display of ornaments, pot plants, knick-knacks, wall decorations and well-polished furniture must have kept the housemaids very busy, yet the décor probably made patrons – whose own drawing rooms at home aspired to look much the same – feel at ease.

Beginning as a laird's settlement, Kingussie grew to become the capital of Badenoch, having Police Burgh status and a court by 1867. At the corner of High Street and King Street, Wolfenden's turreted Star Hotel of 1892 can be seen on the right. Almost opposite is the Royal Hotel. In the 1890s much reconstruction was carried out, based on the original feuing plan of 1799. Shops and services were developing – grocers, butchers, chemists, drapers, launderers, stationers and banks had all appeared – supplying local needs and those of visitors. The buildings on the right housed the coach office for the Tulloch & Loch Laggan mail coach service.

SPEY STREET, KINGUSSIE

Spey Street in Kingussie runs parallel to the High Street on its east side. This 1913 view from the bridge over the River Gynack looks north and shows some notable structures. On the left, beyond the corner building containing the Bank of Scotland (and which now houses the Abbeyfield sheltered accommodation complex), are St Columba's Episcopal Church (1903) and the Victoria Hall (1888), followed by a variety of houses with gardens opposite. The post office of 1909, designed by Alexander Cattanach, was also in Spey Street and a postman with his bicycle is seen on the bridge. The new Badenoch Community Centre, opened in 2003, combines the old hall site and the former church.

HIGH STREET, KINGUSSIE

Copyright.
Ksc. 27

Looking north along Kingussie's High Street in the latter 1920s reveals that motor cars had by that time become both affordable and popular, although horse-drawn vehicles continued in use. An Austin 7 van is outside a draper's while an assortment of saloons and tourers show that the visitors had arrived. The crow-stepped building on the left is the branch of the British Linen Bank, formerly the Caledonian Bank, designed by Matthews & Lawrie in 1875/76 and now the Bank of Scotland. The late-Victorian phase of reconstruction replaced many older structures on this busy street, which by the time of this photograph had become part of the A9 Great North Road.

Kingussie's Cross is formed by the junction of the High Street with King Street and Ardbrullach Road (facing). The Roma Café was opened in 1929 by Bernardo Capaldi, an Italian confectioner who served ice cream and teas. Many Italians had such premises – noted for their marble and chrome interiors – in Scottish towns where they became very popular. Mr Capaldi is seen here outside his premises (now the Café Volante) and his name is remembered in the Capaldi Cup, a competition in the local welfare association football league. The Clock Tower beside East Terrace dates from 1925 and was gifted to the burgh by John D. MacGruer, a local man and New Zealand émigré.

In 1901 the Grampian Sanatorium, designed by local architect Alexander Mackenzie, was opened by Dr Walter de Watteville, a Swiss physician based in Kingussie. The only private facility of its kind in Britain, it treated patients suffering from pulmonary tuberculosis. Fresh, pine-scented air was thought beneficial until the advent of antibiotics in the 1950s finally put the scourge of TB under control. Dr de Watteville also pioneered the use of hydro-electricity from the River Gynack to provide for the facility. In 1934 the Sisters of the Order of Charity of St Vincent de Paul became owners, and it is now a community nursing home for the elderly run by the Highland Health Board.

Golf has been played at Kingussie since 1891. The course on springy moorland turf is high above the town with views to the Cairngorms. Before the First World War, Harry Vardon, the champion golfer, gave advice about extending the course to 18 holes. It is now one of the finest inland courses in the Highlands. In 1904, a clubhouse in the Arts & Crafts style was designed by local architect Alexander Mackenzie. It is seen here beyond the putting green and pay hut. The clubhouse was much enlarged in 1911 and again in 1980, but the putting green is now part of a caravan park.

Pitmain Lodge, a prominent landmark near Glen Gynack, was built around 1913 for James Douglas Fletcher, a wealthy landowner of Rosehaugh in the Black Isle who had bought Pitmain estate. His father, who belonged to Elgin, had made his money in Liverpool's import trade with South America in wool for cloth manufacture from alpaca and other species. Constructed of English red brick, the lodge was reckoned an eyesore but the interiors were lined with fine panelling in oak, teak, pine and walnut, and the building had 364 windows. Occupied in the Second World War by the military, it survived until 1957 when it was demolished. A new lodge has since been erected on the site.

Badenoch is a stronghold of shinty, an ancient community game resembling Irish hurling. Teams of 12 players armed with wooden camans try to score 'hails', or goals, in fast and furious combat for 90 minutes. In 1893 the Camanachd Association was formed in Kingussie to advance the game and the Camanachd Cup championship followed in 1896. In 1903 Kingussie were declared the winners after an inconclusive draw with Inveraray at Perth. Although local rivals Newtonmore have a record of 28 wins in the cup competition, Kingussie had a run of 20 consecutive championships up to 2006. The game is now encouraged in Highland schools among both boys and girls.

The Seaforth Highlanders originated in 1778 with the 72nd Highlanders raised by the Earl of Seaforth, which became the Duke of Albany's Own Highlanders in 1823. In 1793 the 78th Highlanders, Ross-shire Buffs, were raised by Colonel Francis H. Mackenzie, and in 1881 both were amalgamated as the Seaforth Highlanders. With a depot at Fort George, the Seaforths' recruiting territory stretched from Moray to Orkney and they took part in 'wars of Empire' from India to South Africa. Nine regular, territorial and service battalions served in the First World War; the regiment lost over 8,000 men in the conflict. When this photograph was taken in 1908 the 5th Battalion – with men from Caithness and Sutherland – was in camp near Kingussie. The Seaforth name disappeared entirely in the army amalgamations of 2006.

Influenced by Scandinavian 'open air' museums in the 1920s, Dr Isabel F. Grant began collecting Highland artefacts to save 'the old settings of daily life'. These were stored on Iona and in 1939 came to Laggan. In 1943, she bought the former Pitmain Lodge in Kingussie and established Am Fasgadh ('The Shelter'), opening it as the Highland Folk Museum. In the grounds, houses were reconstructed, including a Lewis 'blackhouse' (left), which survives, an Inverness-shire cottage (centre) and a 'but and ben' (right). Dr Grant retired in 1954 but the 'living history' for which she worked can be seen to advantage at the enlarged Highland Folk Museum at Newtonmore.

Between 1790 and 1796 Balavil House was designed and built by Robert and John Adam for James Macpherson. Formerly a local schoolmaster at Ruthven, he was 'translator' (or probably author) of the poems of Ossian, based on Gaelic legends, and this brought him fame and fortune. While publication in 1761 raised questions over his sources, it also helped to promote the Romantic Movement, bringing the first tourists to see Highland landscapes and to appreciate Gaelic culture. The house was destroyed by fire and rebuilt in 1904/05 but its classical finesse has been impaired by this reconstruction. Balavil has recently been used as a setting in the TV series *The Monarch of the Glen*.

The township or clachan of Easter Raitts was cleared in the early nineteenth century in the cause of estate improvement organised by its landlord, James Macpherson of Balavil and of 'Ossian' fame. Its people were resettled in the hamlet of Lynchat, seen here, by the side of the Telford road north of Kingussie and, unusually, the residents have always been 'owner-occupiers'. In recent years excavations have taken place at Baile Gean near Raitts, providing information used in the reconstruction of an eighteenth-century township for the Highland Folk Museum at Newtonmore. Thankfully for Lynchat residents the A9 trunk route now bypasses it.

SPEY BRIDGE AND KINCRAIG

'Ferries' or fords were once the means of crossing the River Spey. This timber bridge at Kincraig, designed by Alexander Mackenzie of Kingussie, dates from 1896 when it probably replaced an earlier structure at the Boat of Insh, as Kincraig was originally known. The bridge had to withstand the passage of ice floes from Loch Insh and has since been renovated and strengthened. From 1863 onwards, lairds encouraged transport links from their estates to the railway. Better communications brought visitors and soon villas, a hotel, two churches – Free (1851) and United Free (1909) – and a nine-hole golf course gave Kincraig village status (the golf course had gone by 1970 however).

Before the railway came, Royal Mail coaches drawn by horses conveyed letters but in 1863 the railway won the contract and post offices were established near stations. Until the 1950s Kincraig was a pick up and dropping off point for mailbags, with line-side apparatus beside the station. The local postmen were responsible for operation of this when, twice daily, the 'Mail Train' raced through with the TPO – the Travelling Post Office – in which letters were sorted in transit. In 1903, around the time of this photograph, the post office at Kincraig was also a general store and the hub of the village.

Before the Inverness & Perth Junction Railway opened in 1863, there was discussion about where stations should be located. Boat of Insh was a chosen site but in 1871 the name was changed to Kincraig after an imposing house close by. As the railway was a single-track system, there had to be many places or 'loops' for trains to pass – Kincraig was one of these. On 3 May 1965 the station was closed, the simple timber buildings removed and the stationmaster's house and cottages sold off, but the passing place remains on the line.

Insh is a crofting township whose origins stem from the resettlement of people from Glen Feshie, moved to make way for sheep rearing and sporting activities in the early nineteenth century. Just to the west are the Spey Meadows, extensive marshes formed by the ponding back of river water by a huge delta of debris brought down by the present River Feshie and earlier meltwater streams from the Cairngorm ice sheets. This phenomenon also created Loch Insh. The Insh Marshes are a National Nature Reserve managed by the Royal Society for the Protection of Birds. The township's name is also associated with the sixth-century foundation of a church by Celtic missionaries on a mound beside Loch Insh. The mound has been used as a place of worship continuously since that time and is now the site of Insh Church, which has a sacred hand-bell of Celtic origin. There is also a small church in Insh village.

Loch Alvie is famed for its fishings, notably of pike. In 1786 a Colonel Thomas Thornton of Yorkshire apparently landed one over six feet in length. The bridge seen here was built around 1814, a time when the Commission for Highland Roads and Bridges – with Thomas Telford as engineer – was improving many Highland routes. A concrete structure replaced it in the mid 1920s.

Alvie estate, for long a property of the Macpherson-Grants, was bought in 1876 by Sir John Ramsden, owner of Ardverikie. This view shows the lodge before reconstruction in 1908 by the architect W.L. Carruthers of Inverness. In 1927 Alvie became the home of the Williamson family. Although a sporting estate, it has interests in farming, forestry and quarrying; the present laird, Jamie Williamson, has also established a fish hatchery and horse riding, quad biking and clay pigeon shooting facilities, in addition to a caravan and chalet park.